FOOD AND CELEBRATIONS
GERMANY

Sylvia Goulding

WAYLAND

This edition published in 2008 by Wayland
(a division of Hachette Children's Books)

Wayland
Hachette Children's Books
338 Euston Road
London NW1 3BH

Wayland Australia
Level 17/207 Kent Street
Sydney NSW 2000

© 2008 The Brown Reference Group plc

The Brown Reference Group plc
First Floor
9–17 St. Albans Place
London N1 0NX
www.brownreference.com

ISBN-13: 978-0-750256-35-3

Printed in Dubai

Wayland is a division of Hachette Children's Books, an Hachette Livre UK Company.
www.hachettelivre.co.uk

10 9 8 7 6 5 4 3 2 1

Photographic Credits:
Front and Back Cover: Klaus Arras
Fotolia: 6; **Ewald Gerlach:** 8, 13; **Michael Gerlach:** 7; **Thomas Gerlach:** 22, 23, 39; **Mike Goulding:** 31; **Peter Hillebrand:** 20/21; **iStock:** title page, 34; **Shutterstock:** 3, 5, 6, 9, 10, 12, 13, 26, 28, 29, 30, 37, 38, 40, 41, 42

With thanks to models:
Anouk, Caspar, Gero, Jamila, Simon

Cooking Editor

Angelika Ilies has always been interested in cookery and other countries. She studied nutritional sciences in college. She has lived in the United States, England and Germany. She has also traveled extensively and collected international recipes on her journeys. Angelika has written more than 70 cookbooks and cooking card series. She currently lives in Frankfurt, Germany, with her two children and has spent much time researching children's nutrition. Both children regularly cook with their mother.

Project Editor: Sylvia Goulding
Cooking Editor: Angelika Ilies
Contributors: Jacqueline Fortey, Sylvia Goulding
Photographers: Klaus Arras, Angelika Ilies,
    Emanuelle Morgan, Dirk Scholz
Cartographer: Darren Awuah
Art Editor: Paula Keogh
Illustrator: Jo Gracie
Picture Researcher: Mike Goulding
Managing Editor: Bridget Giles
Production Director: Alastair Gourlay
Editorial Director: Lindsey Lowe
Children's Publisher: Anne O'Daly

Contents

let's
START COOKING

Cooking is fun – you learn about different ingredients and cooking methods, you find out how things taste, and you can serve to your family and friends a meal that you have cooked yourself! Some of the recipes in this book have steps that need adult help – ask a parent or other adult if they will be your kitchen assistant while you cook a meal.

This line tells you how many people the meal will feed.

In this box, you find out which ingredients you need for your meal.

WHAT YOU NEED:

SERVES 4 PEOPLE:

500g white rice
4 eggs, beaten
light soy sauce
4 tablespoons
    groundnut or
    soy oil
2 spring onions
50g peeled prawns
50g ham
50g peas

Check before you start that you have everything at home. If something is missing, write it on your shopping list. Get all the ingredients ready before you start cooking.

◁ I enjoy preparing all the fresh vegetables. I wash, trim, peel and de-seed them, if necessary. Then I slice and chop them all to the same size.

! WHEN TO GET help

Most cooking involves cutting ingredients and heating them in some way, whether frying, boiling or cooking in the oven. Each time you see this exclamation mark, be extra careful as you cook and make sure your adult kitchen assistant is around to help.

For many meals you need to chop an onion. First cut off a thin slice at both ends. Pull off the peel. Cut the onion in half from end to end. Put one half with the cut side down on the chopping board. Hold it with one hand and cut end-to-end slices with the other hand. Hold the slices together and cut across the slices to make small cubes. Make sure you do not cut yourself!

For other recipes in this book you need to make a dough. Put the ingredients into a bowl and knead them with very clean hands or with the kneading hooks of a hand-held whisk. In many cases, the recipe then tells you to cover the bowl with a clean cloth and to leave it in a warm place. During this time, the dough rises – that is, it gets bigger. After rising, knead the dough again until smooth.

A **barbecue** is not essential, but in summer German people enjoy cooking their meals outdoors.

Oven gloves are essential in any kitchen. Wear them each time you touch a dish on the hob or in the oven.

Pepper mills are a useful tool to have in any kitchen, because pepper tastes much better when it is freshly ground.

A **rolling pin** is a handy kitchen tool for rolling out the dough when you are making cakes, breads or biscuits.

A trip around
GERMANY

After World War II (1939–45), Germany was divided into two countries. In 1990, West Germany and East Germany reunited to become one state again.

Germany is in the heart of Europe. It is much larger than the United Kingdom and is divided into sixteen federal lands. Germany borders the North Sea and the Baltic Sea in the north. Its northern border with Denmark crosses a spit of land called Jutland. Germany's western neighbours are Holland, Belgium, Luxembourg and France.

▽ **About 82 million people** live in Germany. About ten percent of these are immigrants. They came from Turkey, Greece, Italy, Poland, Russia, Serbia, Croatia and Spain.

Switzerland and Austria are to the south, and the Czech Republic and Poland to the east.

Northern Germany forms part of the North European Plain. In the centre of the country, the land becomes hillier. In the south, it rises higher still in the Bavarian Alps. The Rhine is Europe's longest river and busiest waterway. It flows through the west of the country, from the Swiss Alps to the North Sea. In the east, the River Elbe crosses Germany to the Baltic Sea. Many industries are located in a heavily built-up region around coalfields in the east.

NORTH AMERICA

ASIA

EUROPE — GERMANY

AFRICA

◁ **Germany** is a large country in central Europe. Its population is the largest in the European Union. It shares borders with nine other countries.

DENMARK

BALTIC SEA

1

△ **Sandy beaches** line the Baltic and North Sea coasts. The beaches in the east are quiet. Straw baskets protect people from the sea breeze.

NORTH SEA

GREAT BRITAIN

Hamburg

Elbe

LÜNEBURG HEATH

1

NETHERLANDS

Hannover

GERMANY

3

POLAND

BERLIN

SAXONY

Dresden

4

BELGIUM

Cologne
Bonn

Rhine

2

Leipzig

4

CZECH REPUBLIC

△ **Cochem Castle** is a fairytale castle on the River Moselle. It is 1,000 years old.

Frankfurt

BAVARIA

Stuttgart

Danube

△ **Dresden** is the capital of Saxony. It was once the residence of the kings of Saxony. The Zwinger *(above)* is a complex of pavilions and galleries built in 1711–22.

FRANCE

Munich

SWITZERLAND ⤝ LIECHTENSTEIN

AUSTRIA

SLOVAKIA

HUNGARY

◁ **Berlin** is the capital of Germany. It is located in the east of the country, about 160 kilometres from the Polish border. The Brandenburg Gate is one of its best-known landmarks. It once stood on the border between east and west.

SLOVENIA

CROATIA

BOSNIA-HERZEGOVINA

3

ITALY

MEDITERRANEAN SEA

Northern Germany

Germany has many beautiful sandy beaches. On the North Sea coast, large mudflats appear when the tide goes out. A string of small islands, the East and North Frisian Islands, are just off the coast. Germany's largest island is Rügen on the Baltic coast.

The rolling northern plain contains marshes and moors, dotted with lakes and ponds. There is fertile soil for farming towards the uplands farther south. The large port of Hamburg stands on the banks of the River Elbe.

Central Germany

The central uplands form a band across the middle of the country. The Harz mountain range is the most northerly mountain chain. Its higher slopes are covered with pine trees. The River Main winds its way across Germany until it joins the Rhine farther west. A cruise along the Rhine passes through spectacular

△ **A tall sailing ship** called a *windjammer* in the port of Hamburg during the Port Festival. Hamburg Harbour is the largest seaport in Germany and the second largest in Europe. Hamburg is located 112 kilometres inland from the mouth of the River Elbe .

scenery. In the Middle Ages (about 500–1500 CE), people built castles and fortresses here to guard and control this waterway.

On the terraced slopes of the Rhine, Main and Moselle excellent vines are grown. Old volcanic craters in the Eifel Mountains are filled with bright blue water. Other mountain ranges include the Taunus near Frankfurt and the Erzgebirge on the Czech border.

Southern Germany

The Black Forest takes its name from the dense, dark woods of pine and fir that cover its hills. It is a picturesque region in the south-western state of Baden-Württemberg. Tourists come here to enjoy the scenery and walk the tracks. The River Danube rises in the Black Forest and flows eastwards across Bavaria.

The Bavarian capital, Munich, is famous for culture, food, brewing and beer festivals. Lake Constance is a large lake on the Rhine, formed by a glacier many years ago. The Bavarian Alps are spectacular. The highest alpine peaks are in France, but Germany's highest mountain, the Zugspitze, reaches 2,962 metres.

▽ *Neuschwanstein Castle* near Füssen in Bavaria was built in the 19th century for King Ludwig II. It is Germany's most popular tourist site and became the model for Disneyland's castles.

LAPTOPS & LEDERHOSEN

Bavaria is famous for its folk costumes. Men wear leather shorts or three-quarter length trousers called 'lederhosen', women wear 'dirndl' skirts with white blouses and aprons. But there is much more to Bavaria than tradition. Large companies are based here, such as the car manufacturers BMW and Audi, the engineering company Siemens, Airbus Industries and many other high-tech companies.

The food we grow in
GERMANY

Germany has short coastlines, but fruit and vegetables grow well, and rich meadows provide food for livestock.

Germany is renowned as a country of meat-eaters. But fruit and vegetables also grow well here, and people love locally grown and seasonal fresh foods.

Northern plains

South of the North Sea and Baltic coasts, Germany has vast moorland areas. Here, sheep, bees and berry bushes flourish. The Lüneburg Heath in Lower Saxony is especially famous for its heather honey. Lower Saxony's Altes Land is an important centre for growing fruit. Sugarbeet, potatoes and corn, which are grown as cattle fodder, are also important northern crops.

The city of Hamburg has market gardens nearby to supply it with fruit and vegetables, such as cabbages and carrots. In the southern part of the northern plains, the soil is more fertile. Wheat, barley, corn and sugarbeet grow well here. There are also many dairy and poultry farms across northern Germany. The black-and-white Friesian cows are particularly famous. The farms often produce their own cheeses, sausages and other products.

Central uplands

Highland soils are not as fertile as those found in river valleys, but farmers grow some cereal crops in upland areas. This region of the country is also good for growing potatoes and vegetables. Potatoes are very popular in Germany. They are boiled, or used to make pancakes, salads or fried potato dishes.

People keep pigs for pork products, such as ham and sausages. Dairy cows graze on hillside pastures, and beef cattle are reared for their meat. There are also small poultry farms that keep chickens, geese and ducks.

Farming is intensive along the large and densely populated river valleys of the Rhine and Main. The land has to produce a large amount of food and so farmers often use fertilizers. But today people demand more and more organic food. Market gardens grow fruit and vegetables for people living in nearby cities, such as Cologne and Bonn.

◁ **Vast fields** of wheat, rye and barley stretch across the plains in northern and eastern Germany. These cereals are ground and then used by bakers to make about 300 different types of bread.

Vines are grown in terraces along the steep, warm, protected hillsides of the Rhine, Moselle, Nahe and Ahr rivers. They produce grapes for Germany's white wines.

In the east, the butchers of Thuringia have perfected the art of sausage making – its fried sausages are sold around the country. Large poultry farms in Saxony rear geese for the traditional German Christmas dinner.

The south

Hops are used to give beer its special flavour. People have been growing hops in Hallertau in Bavaria for more than a thousand years, and it is now the world's largest hop-growing area. Southern Germany also has orchards and vineyards. Apples are grown around Lindau, on the shores of Lake Constance.

The land of Baden-Württemberg is Germany's most southerly wine-growing area.

In mid-April, growers start to harvest the white asparagus. It thrives in the sandy soil of Baden-Württemberg. Asparagus is treated as a delicacy. During its short season, the restaurants all have special asparagus menus.

In the Saarland, in Germany's far west, plums are a speciality, particularly a variety called Zwetschgen or quetsches. They are made into large trays of juicy plum cake.

▽ **As soon as the snows melt**, temporary farmers take the cows up to the higher mountain pastures for the summer. The grass can recover in the valleys until the cows are taken back down in the autumn.

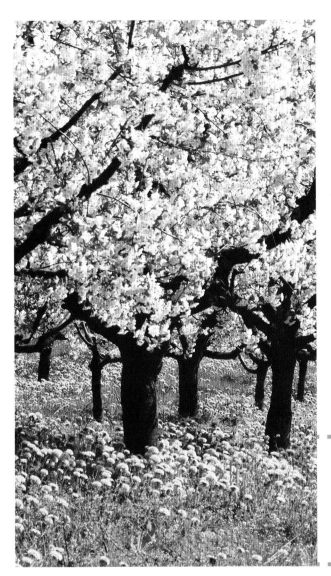

In Franconia, the northern part of Bavaria, growers cultivate sweet cherries. Apples are made into juice and tasty apple strudel. People put cherries in a rich chocolate cake called Black Forest gateau. The West Allgäu in Bavaria is known for its cheeses.

Fishing

Fishermen catch herrings, mackerel, cod, sardines and prawns in the North Sea, the Baltic and the Atlantic. Fried fillets of plaice are a famous dish from Hamburg. Where rivers and lakes are less polluted, freshwater fish are on the increase. Germans eat freshwater fish, such as trout, pike, carp, perch and zander. Carp was once a favourite new year's dish.

◁ **Cherry trees** are in full blossom in a wildflower meadow. Germany is one of the most important cherry producers. The fruits grow especially well in the west and south. Cherries are eaten as fruit and are used to make juices, cakes and kirsch.

COAST GUARDS

The North Sea dykes were built from clay and covered in grass hundreds of years ago. The coast guards keep 'dyke sheep' to help maintain the dykes, which protect the land from high tides. The sheep trample down the soil without tearing up the grass and 'mow' the grass by eating it.

let's make...
FRIED PLAICE

This dish comes from Finkenwerder, which is a part of the city of Hamburg in northern Germany. Fishing boats from here once went all over the North Sea and the Norwegian Sea.

WHAT YOU NEED:

SERVES 4 PEOPLE:

4 plaice, gutted and ready
  to cook (each weighing
  about 375g)
salt, white pepper
2–3 tablespoons plain flour
150g bacon (optional)
50g butter
1 untreated organic lemon
fresh dill

◁ This fish tastes good with almost any kind of potato dish. Try frying the potatoes with a few onion rings, or boil them in their skins, then peel them and add fresh parsley. Another great side dish is a cucumber salad.

I CAN'T FIND ANY _plaice_

You can also make this dish with another flat fish, such as sole. Or use any other fish fillet.

MY TIP

A tasty version of this recipe uses tiny North Sea prawns. Fry these briefly with the bacon in butter. Then sprinkle them over the top of the plaice.

1 Thoroughly wash the plaice under cold water, then pat them dry with kitchen towels. Season them with salt and pepper, then dust each one thinly with flour on both sides.

2 Use two wide frying pans so you can cook all four fillets at the same time. Finely chop the bacon. Put half the bacon and half the butter into each frying pan. Fry the bacon over a medium heat until it is crispy.

3 Put the plaice into the frying pans side by side. Fry over a medium heat for about 4 minutes, then turn over. Fry for 4 more minutes.

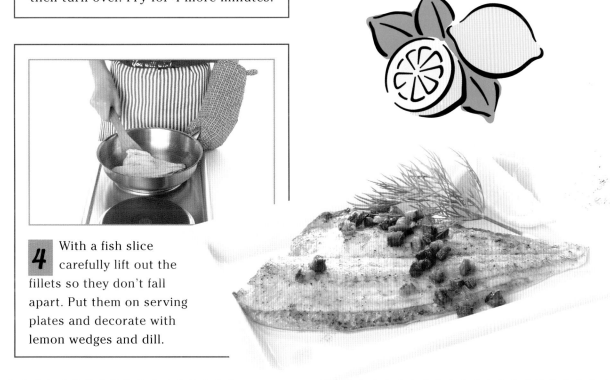

4 With a fish slice carefully lift out the fillets so they don't fall apart. Put them on serving plates and decorate with lemon wedges and dill.

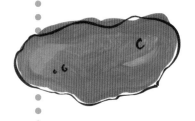

let's make...
POTATO PANCAKES

Potato pancakes are a speciality of the Rhineland, especially of Cologne. They are sold from stands at funfairs and festivals, and people eat them strolling around.

WHAT YOU NEED:

SERVES 4 PEOPLE:

1.2kg starchy potatoes
2 onions
just under 125ml sour cream
4 eggs
about 50g dried breadcrumbs
salt, black pepper
vegetable oil for frying

◁ I love this pancake the traditional way, served with apple sauce. But my aunt prefers the savoury version. She eats hers with smoked salmon.

WHAT SORT OF <u>potatoes</u>?

Starchy potatoes work best for pancakes. Try King Edward or white potatoes.

MY TIP

Try this pancake on a slice of pumpernickel, or black bread, with some golden syrup – this is the version loved in the hilly areas around Cologne.

16

1 Wash and peel the potatoes, then grate them either finely or coarsely – whichever you prefer.

2 Squeeze out the grated potatoes, either with your hands or in a clean teatowel. Put the 'dry' potato pulp into a bowl.

3 Peel and finely grate the onions. Add them to the potatoes. Add the sour cream, eggs, breadcrumbs and a little salt and pepper. Stir or knead everything together.

4 In a wide frying pan, heat plenty **!** of oil over a medium heat. You need plenty of oil as the potatoes soak it up.

5 To make a pancake, put one **!** heaped tablespoon of potato mix into the frying pan. Pat it flat with the back of a large spoon. Fry the pancake for 3–4 minutes, then turn it over and fry for another 3–4 minutes, until both sides are crispy and golden brown.

6 Lift out finished pancakes and let them drain on kitchen towels while you cook the rest. Keep them warm in a low oven (100°C or gas mark ½).

let's make...
DUMPLINGS AND MUSHROOMS

Dumplings can be made from bread, as in this recipe, or from potatoes. They are particularly popular in southern Germany, where people eat them with many sauce-based dishes.

▽ This Bavarian dish makes a great vegetarian meal, but it also tastes good with roast pork or goulash.

WHAT YOU NEED:

SERVES 4 PEOPLE:

5 stale bread rolls
salt
250ml milk
½ bunch flat-leaved parsley

½ small onion
1 tablespoon butter
2 eggs

FOR THE MUSHROOM SAUCE:

2 tablespoons dried mushrooms
4 onions
2 tablespoons butter
1 tablespoon plain flour
250ml vegetable stock
125ml single cream
2 teaspoons dried thyme
salt, black pepper

SERVE WITH: _mushroom sauce_

Put the dried mushrooms in a small bowl, cover them with in warm water and leave to soak. Drain and chop the mushrooms but keep the water. Peel and finely chop the onions. Heat the butter in a saucepan and fry the onions until golden. Add the mushrooms and fry for a few minutes. Dust with flour and fry for another minute, then pour in the stock. Add the soaking water and the cream. Season with thyme, salt and pepper. Cook over a gentle heat for 10 minutes.

1 Cut the rolls into very thin slices and put them in a bowl. Sprinkle the slices with ¼ teaspoon salt. In a saucepan, bring the milk to the boil. Pour the milk over the rolls, cover with a clean teatowel and allow to soak for about 30 minutes.

2 Meanwhile wash, pat dry and finely chop the parsley. Peel and finely chop the onion *(see page 5)*. Melt the butter in a frying pan and fry the onion until it is transparent (see-through).

3 Add the onions, parsley and eggs to the soaked bread rolls. Knead everything with your hands until it is a smooth paste. With moist hands, shape the mixture into eight balls.

4 In a large saucepan, bring plenty of water and a little salt to the boil. Reduce the heat and place the dumplings into the saucepan on a slotted spoon. Cook the dumplings over a low heat for about 20 minutes.

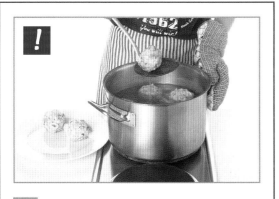

5 Lift the dumplings out of the water with a slotted spoon and drain well. Serve with the mushroom sauce.

How we celebrate in
GERMANY

People in Germany celebrate Christian holidays, the joys of summer and the most important calendar dates.

A s in most western countries, Christian festivals, such as Easter and Christmas, are celebrated all over Germany. Many other religious Christian festivals are only celebrated in some federal areas. This depends on whether there are more Catholic or Protestant citizens in that area. New Year is celebrated everywhere.

Rhine festivals

The summer festival known as 'The Rhine in Flames' is a series of five huge firework displays on the River Rhine. They take place on different dates between May and September. The largest is celebrated in Koblenz on the second Saturday each August.

For each event, long convoys of seventy-five or more ships travel slowly up the Rhine, from Bingen to Bonn. Huge fireworks are set off from the ships. Bengal fires and laser light shows douse the towns and villages along its shore in colourful lights. Hundreds of thousands of people come to see the displays.

A similar event, known as 'Cologne Lights', began in Cologne in 2001. Here, the main two fireworks are set off from two large pontoon

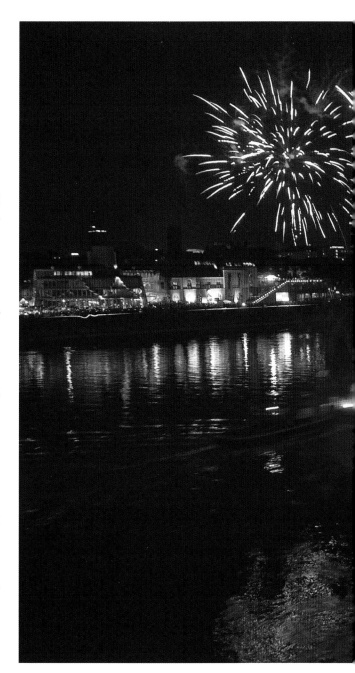

ships in the river. There are more fireworks on the shores. Music is played from huge speakers all along this stretch of the river. The colourful fireworks explode in time to match the rhythm of the music. When the convoy of ships arrives, people light 500,000 sparklers. The atmosphere is very festive.

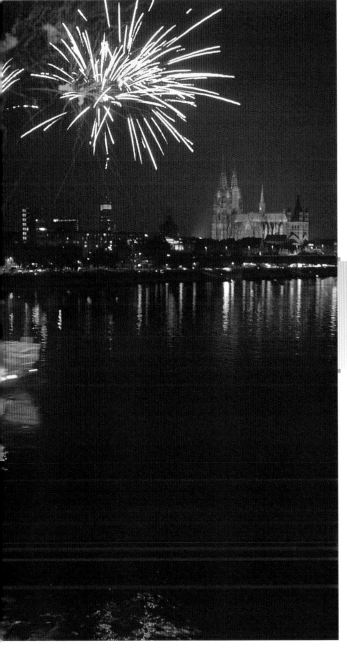

Silvester

Silvester is the name for New Year's Eve in Germany. At midnight, people set off even more fireworks, outside their homes in the street, outside bars or in large open squares.

Doughnuts are a traditional food to eat on New Year's Eve. If people around Berlin make these themselves, they sometimes fill most with jam, but one with mustard. It is a challenge to see if everyone can eat their doughnut without letting on who had the mustard-filled bun!

Another custom is to melt a lump of lead over a candle. People throw the melted lead into a bowl of cold water. It sets in strange shapes, and everyone decides what these look like. A book tells people what this means for their future. If the shape looks like a lot of grass, for example, that means 'lots of money'.

◁ **Ships are lit** in festive colours as fireworks go off all around them on the River Rhine at Cologne – the city's cathedral can be seen on the right. Live bands play on the shore, in time to the fireworks.

BIG FESTIVAL

The largest festival in the world is the Oktoberfest in Munich. It happens at the end of September. It is known as a beer festival, but there are many other events: festival parades, live brass bands and fairground attractions.

Carnival

Carnival is the time before Lent, the time when Christians fast before Easter. It is celebrated all over Germany and known by many different names, including Karneval, Fastnacht and Fasching.

The six days before Ash Wednesday is the time of the 'street carnival'. Everyone dresses in a funny costume, even the adults. There are parades with floats, marching bands and dancers. People on the floats throw sweets and bunches of flowers to the spectators.

The carnival clubs in each town elect their 'rulers', often a prince and princess, for one season. There are many balls and so-called sessions, or shows. Comedians make speeches, and there are dance performances and many carnival songs for everyone to sing.

△ **The Prince** (with long pheasant feathers), the Peasant (with a fan of peacock feathers) and the Maid (not seen, a man in a woman's dress and with blond plaits) 'rule' in Cologne.

△ **May trees** decorate many houses on 1 May. The tree is usually a birch, which has young leaves at this time of year. Ribbons are made from crêpe paper or silk. Their many different colours once had special meanings.

May Day

Labour Day, 1 May, is a national holiday in Germany. Labour unions organize processions and speeches on that day. But there are many other traditions connected with that day.

The night before, 30 April, is Walpurgisnacht, the night of the witches. Traditionally, people had bonfires to burn the 'bad spirits'. Today, people sing and dance together through the night, the so-called 'dance into May'.

In southern Germany, people parade with a brass band to the village square. There they put up a *Maibaum*, or May tree. This is a tall pole or fir tree from which coloured ribbons hang. People hold the other end of the ribbons, and sing and dance around the May pole.

In other areas, people hang a May tree outside their homes. This is a tree or branch, often a birch, that is beautifully decorated with colourful ribbons. In the past, young men put a May tree outside the window of their beloved. It was left there for a month. Then the young woman let her admirer know if she liked him too. Today, people hang these colourful trees as joyful decorations for their houses and to welcome the spring.

let's make...
CHRISTMAS STOLLEN

There are many recipes for stollen. Some have a marzipan filling, some are made with poppy seeds. The famous Dresden stollen is made with quark, a German soft cheese.

WHAT YOU NEED:

MAKES 1 STOLLEN:

475g ricotta cheese, or
   450g cream cheese plus
   3 tablespoons buttermilk)
50g softened butter
1 pinch salt
170g granulated sugar
1 teaspoon vanilla extract
2 eggs

1 teaspoon grated zest
   from an untreated
   lemon
85g soft dried apricots
85g raisins
85g shelled pistachios
85g chopped almonds
450g plain flour
4 teaspoons baking powder

PLUS:

flour for the work surface
butter for brushing
75g icing sugar,

to sprinkle

◁ One slice of this cake is never enough for me!

WHY DOES THIS CAKE HAVE A *dent?*

Traditionally, this Christmas cake is made by folding the dough over and over. This is why it has a dent. The folding symbolizes the swaddling clothes of the baby Jesus.

1 Put the ricotta cheese into a sieve and drain for about 20 minutes. Heat the oven to 180°F (gas mark 4). Line a baking tray with baking paper.

2 Put the butter, salt, sugar, vanilla extract and eggs into a bowl and beat with a hand-held mixer until foamy. Knead in the ricotta cheese. Finely chop and add the apricots, raisins, pistachios, almonds and lemon zest.

3 In a separate bowl, mix the baking powder into the flour. Beat this mixture into the cheese mixture, a bit at a time. Knead until you have a smooth dough. Add a little more flour if necessary – the dough should be smooth, soft and elastic, not sticky. **!**

4 On a floured surface, shape the dough into a loaf with a lengthways dent running down the centre. Place the loaf on a baking tray. Bake in the centre of the oven for about 1 hour. **!**

5 Melt the butter. Take the stollen out of the oven and brush with the butter. Thickly sprinkle the cake with icing sugar and allow to cool on a rack. **!**

let's make...
MUTZENMANDELN

Mutzenmandeln are a favourite carnival pastry. Like pancakes on Shrove Tuesday or Mardi Gras, people make these little biscuits to use up eggs and fat before the start of Lent.

▽ At my last carnival party, Dad dressed up as a clown and brought freshly baked mutzenmandeln for us all.

WHAT YOU NEED:

MAKES ABOUT 50 MUTZENMANDELN:

225g plain flour
85g shelled and ground almonds
1 teaspoon baking powder
3 eggs
115g cold butter

1 pinch salt
a pinch each of ground cinnamon, ground cardamom and grated lemon zest

PLUS:

oil for deep-frying
icing sugar for dusting

WHAT'S THIS: Lent?

In Christian tradition, the time before Easter is called Lent. In the past, it was a time for fasting for Christians. They were not allowed to eat meat, fish, eggs or fat. Lent lasts for forty days, from Ash Wednesday to Easter, not counting Sundays.

1 In a bowl, stir together the flour, almonds and baking powder. Add the eggs, butter and the spices and knead to a smooth dough.

2 Shape the dough into a ball. Wrap it in clingfilm and chill for at least 1 hour in the fridge.

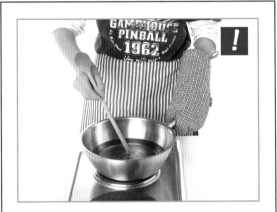

3 Heat the oil for deep-frying. Put a wooden spoon in the oil. If the bubbles rise on the stem immediately, the oil is hot enough.

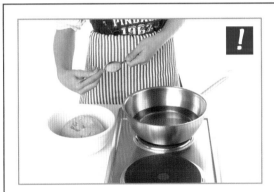

4 Using two teaspoons, take a small portion of dough from the ball and form it into an almond shape. Deep-fry a few at a time in the hot oil for about 1–2 minutes, until they are a golden brown colour. Lift the mutzenmandeln out with a slotted spoon and drain them on kitchen towels. Sprinkle them with icing sugar and allow to cool.

How we celebrate at home in
GERMANY

Family celebrations are very important in Germany. Families are often small, with only one or two children. So people like to celebrate with all their relatives if they can – aunts, uncles, cousins and grandparents.

Christmas

Germany is world-famous for its Christmas celebrations. Many customs that are now common in other countries originally came from Germany.

The four weeks before Christmas are called *Advent*. Children have calendars with a countdown to Christmas. Each day until 24 December, they open one door, and there are often chocolates inside. The family has an advent wreath of pine twigs and cones with four candles. Four Sundays before Christmas they light one candle, three Sundays before they light two, until all are lit the last Sunday before Christmas Day. When the candles are lit, the family sit together and eat their *stollen*, a Christmas cake.

◁ **Santa Claus** comes on Christmas Eve. He knocks on the door as most German houses do not have a chimney for him to slide down. Often he reads from a golden book that tells him whether a child has been good or not.

Most towns have a Christmas market, and large towns even have several markets. There people can buy gifts, decorations for their Christmas trees, candles, handmade toys, sweets and cakes.

Christmas trees in Germany are usually real pine trees. In the past, people stuck real candles to the branches on special candlesticks. Today, fewer people do this because of the fire risks. Festive lights adorn the shops, but usually not people's homes and gardens.

Children's days

German families celebrate Christian events in a child's life. Most children are baptized, often very soon after birth. Between the ages of six and twelve, Catholic children receive their first communion. Protestant children are confirmed after two years of afternoon classes at church when they are fourteen.

An important day in every child's life is the first day of school. The parents and other relatives accompany the child to school. After the first lessons, the child is given a *Schultüte* (say 'shool-toote'). This is a large cardboard cone filled with sweets and toys.

▽ **The first day of school** is an important day in a child's life. To 'sweeten' this start of a life of learning, children are given a cone filled with sweets and other gifts by their parents or grandparents.

ST MARTIN

St Martin was a Roman soldier and later the bishop of Tours. He was a kind man – legend tells us that he cut his coat in half to share it with a beggar in a snow storm. Today, the saint is remembered on the eve of 11 November. German children carry paper lanterns with lit candles in a procession. They knock on people's doors and sing special St Martin's songs. As a reward they are given sweets.

Easter

Many Easter traditions originally came from Germany. People celebrate with painted Easter eggs and chocolate bunnies. Children help paint the eggs. Branches of trees with spring leaves are hung with decorated eggs. Often the parents hide little nests with sweets in the garden or home. The children get up early on Sunday morning to try and find them.

Some traditional foods are eaten for Easter. Maundy Thursday is known as *Gründonnerstag* or green Thursday, so people eat green foods, such as Savoy cabbage. The main Good Friday meal is fish, and on Easter Sunday people often eat lamb.

△ *For their birthdays*, people often invite family and friends over in the afternoon. They have coffee or hot chocolate and a big birthday cake.

Kaffee und Kuchen

When people in Germany get together, they invite each other for *Kaffee und Kuchen*, or coffee and cake. The cake may be bought at a patisserie. But many people bake their own cakes, fruit tarts and biscuits. For family birthdays, especially, a birthday cake is baked and presented to the person whose birthday it is. Coffee and cake are taken in the afternoon. Often people use their best china.

Weddings

German couples do not traditionally have a stag or hen party. Instead, they spend the evening before the wedding at the bride's home. Friends and neighbours come around and smash their old china on the stairs. The couple has to sweep up the shards. The noise is meant to chase away bad spirits, and tidying up together prepares the couple for a lifetime of working together when they are married.

At the wedding party, relatives may kidnap the bride and take her to a nearby bar. Once the bridegroom has noticed that his new wife is missing, he goes to find her. As a 'ransom' he pays for everything the bride and her abductors have eaten or drunk in the meantime.

▽ **Polterabend**, or 'noisy evening', is the evening before a wedding. Friends visit and smash their old china. The couple sweep it up together, but a mischievous friend may empty the dustbin again and again!

let's make...
SAUERBRATEN

This marinated casserole is our family's favourite Sunday meal. It takes a few days to make so we don't eat it every day. We often eat it with potato dumplings and red cabbage.

WHAT YOU NEED:

SERVES 4-6 PEOPLE:

1 onion
1 carrot
1 stick celery
150ml wine vinegar
5 cloves
½ teaspoon allspice berries
1 teaspoon juniper berries
1.2kg brisket, flank or
    topside of beef
2 tablespoons lard or oil
75g gingerbread
pieces
1–2 handfuls raisins
1–3 tablespoons syrup
½ carton crème fraîche
salt, black pepper

◁ On Sundays, we all sit together and enjoy this dish. My parents thought it was great when I made sauerbraten all by myself.

WHAT'S THIS: <u>sauerbraten?</u>

Literally, this means 'sour roast', because the meat is marinated in a sour liquid, with lots of vinegar. In the past, when people had no fridges, that was a way of preserving meat. It also makes tough cuts of meat very tender.

1 Peel the onion and carrot. Trim the celery. Roughly chop all three and put them in a saucepan. Add the vinegar, 600ml water, the cloves, and the allspice and juniper berries. Bring to the boil. Turn off the heat and allow to cool.

!

3 On the day you want to eat the beef, heat the oil in a flameproof casserole. Lift the meat out of the liquid and pat it dry with paper towels. Place it in the oil and fry all around on a high heat to seal. Add half a glass of water to the saucepan. In a sieve, filter about 250ml vinegar marinade and add. Cover and cook over a low heat for 1½ hours.

!

2 Wash the meat under cold water and place it in a narrow, high bowl. Pour over the vinegar mixture. Make sure the meat is completely covered with the liquid. Cover the bowl with a clean teatowel and place it in the fridge for 3–4 days to marinate. Turn the meat over several times during this period.

!

4 Lift out the meat, cover, and keep warm. Finely crumble the gingerbread into the sauce and stir. Stir in the raisins, golden syrup and crème fraîche. Season with pepper and salt. Serve the meat with the sauce.

let's make...
PLUM CAKE

In summer, when lots of fruits ripen, this is one of the nicest ways of using them up. Mum makes plum cake for all summer birthdays – it's large enough for any number of candles!

▽ My grandparents, aunt and uncle are coming over this afternoon for cake and coffee, to celebrate Dad's birthday. I can't wait!

WHAT YOU NEED:

MAKES 20 SLICES:

225g plain flour
1 teaspoon dried yeast
250ml lukewarm milk
1 tablespoon sugar
1 pinch salt
1 egg yolk
1½ tablespoons soft butter
1.75kg firm plums

PLUS:

flour for the work surface
butter for the baking tray
80g almond slices

WHAT SORT OF <u>plums?</u>

The original recipe uses quetsches, a kind of damson. But there are many other types of plums to choose from. They range in size from cherry to apple, and in colour from yellow, green and red to purple. Choose firm plums that have a good flavour and do not contain too much water.

1 Put the flour in a bowl and stir in the yeast and pour over the milk. Sprinkle over a little sugar and flour. Cover with a clean teatowel and stand in a warm place for 15 minutes, until the flour has cracks on the surface. **!**

3 Quickly knead the dough with your hands on a floured surface. Shape it into a ball, dust with flour, cover and allow to rise again in a warm place, until it has become almost twice as big.

4 Wash the plums and halve them or fold them open. Cut out the pits. Heat the oven to 200°C (gas mark 6).

2 Add the salt, egg yolk and soft butter. Using the kneading hooks of a hand-held blender, work it all into a smooth dough. It should easily come away from the bowl and not be sticky.

5 Knead the dough again, then roll it out on a floured surface. Grease the baking tray with a little butter. Lift the dough on to the tray and press and push it out to the edges.

6 Place the plums closely together on the dough. Sprinkle over the almonds. Bake in the centre of the oven for about 30 minutes.

How we live in
GERMANY

Germany is a diverse country, and the people who live there follow many different lifestyles. One thing most people have in common is a love of the outdoors, sports and holidays.

Parks and gardens

In most German towns there are lovely parks, and people love going for a walk in the park. Turkish families in Germany often get together in the park in large groups to have a picnic and barbecue. The parks also attract joggers, dog walkers and children who play in the playgrounds. Many Germans have a garden behind their house or they rent a piece of land elsewhere. They grow beautiful flowers and many gardens have a fish pond. In summer, people invite friends for a barbecue. Gardening is a popular hobby, especially for older people.

▽ **Boat trips** are a favourite entertainment. Cruise ships go up and down Germany's many rivers, such as the Rhine, Danube and Moselle. Evening tours often include music and shows.

△ **Snow falls** in many parts of Germany in winter so everyone can enjoy themselves with snowball fights, making snowmen, tobogganing, ice skating, ice hockey, skiing and snowboarding.

Sports

Germans are sports mad. One in every three of them belongs to a sports club. Their greatest passion is soccer; Germany won the World Cup in 1954, 1974 and 1990. It hosted the matches in 2006. Every village has its club, and people are fiercely loyal to their local club. Another very popular sport is tennis.

There are also swimming pools, both indoor and open-air, in almost every village. People cycle and hike, and in-line skating is popular. All kinds of winter sports, including ski jumping, also have many fans. Millions watch sports events on TV, from soccer matches to motor racing and boxing.

Family life

In large cities, Germans often live in flats in rows of houses. In villages, they may live in a bungalow or a two-family house. Often people rent and do not own their homes.

For breakfast, German families often have a great spread of different foods, especially on Sundays, when no one has to rush off to work or school. There are bowls of cereals and different kinds of bread, including rolls, country breads and sweet loaves. There are different cold meats, hams, and cheeses, all sorts of jams, and boiled eggs.

△ **Hiking trails** make it possible to walk long or short distances anywhere in Germany. People enjoy walking in the hilly mountain regions, climbing the higher peaks or paddling in the mudflats of the North Sea.

People used to have their main meal at lunchtime. In some families this still happens, because children get home from school at this time. But in many families today both parents work, so the main meal is eaten in the evening. The meal can be a casserole of meat, for example a 'false hare'. Other favourites are sausages or meat rissoles – burgers without buns.

The many ethnic groups in Germany have introduced their own dishes, and German children enjoy Italian pasta dishes and pizzas, as well as Turkish doner kebabs or gyros. *Fritten*, or fries, are everyone's favourite.

For dessert people have a blancmange, ice cream or a red dessert called *grütze*. Many Germans today eat fast foods, such as burgers, just like in other Western countries.

School and vacation

Children in Germany start school at the age of six. They attend primary school for four years. After that, they go to one of three types of schools. *Hauptschule* (years 5–9) generally leads to a vocational (or skill-based) school and an apprenticeship. *Realschule* (years 5–10) is a higher vocational school. *Gymnasium* (years 5–13) ends with the *Abitur*. This is the certificate students need to enter college.

The school day starts at 8 A.M. and finishes at 1 or 2 P.M. Children do not eat at school. They have lots of homework to complete at home and very few after-school activities. All children learn English.

▽ **Zoo animals** are important personalities in Germany. Baby animals, like Marlar, the smallest of the elephants below, may even become celebrities. A visit to the zoo is a big draw.

SAVING THE ENVIRONMENT

Germans recycle much of their rubbish. They pay a deposit and return bottles and cans, and they collect paper, plastic and metal in recycling bins. Kitchen and garden waste is composted in the garden. Instead of using plastic carrier bags, people take their own, usually made from cotton.

let's make...
FALSE HARE

This is an old-fashioned children's favourite, and it is not really a hare, but a meatloaf with a hidden surprise! Every region in Germany has its own version, some include sausages too.

WHAT YOU NEED:

SERVES 4 PEOPLE:

3 eggs
2 slices toast
675g mixed minced meat
   (half beef, half pork)
salt, black pepper
2 teaspoons dried oregano
3 tablespoons oil
125ml stock

▽ We love to eat mashed potato and red cabbage or braised cucumbers with this meatloaf. It's also great with a tomato sauce.

WHY IS IT CALLED _false hare?_

Perhaps it was because people pretended that they had a real hare for Sunday lunch. Many German recipes have names that promise something they do not keep – Heaven and Earth, for example, is a mashed potato with a fried liver and apple stew; and _halver hahn_, half a chicken, is in fact just a cheese sandwich!

1 Prick two of the eggs on both ends with a needle. Then place them carefully (with a spoon) into a saucepan of boiling water. Cover and boil for 10 minutes until they are hard. Rinse under cold water and shell.

!

2 Place the toast in a bowl. Pour over some warm water and allow to swell. Squeeze out the bread and put it in a bowl. Add the minced meat and crack in the third egg. Season with salt, pepper and oregano. Knead the mixture thoroughly with your hands.

3 Rinse your hands under cold water, then shape the meat mixture into an oval loaf shape. Flatten the loaf and set the shelled eggs on top. Fold the meat around the them so they are completely enclosed.

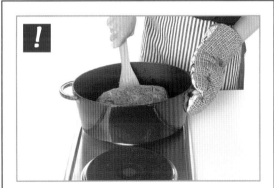

!

4 Heat the oil in an ovenproof casserole. Add the meatloaf. Fry and turn it for 5 minutes to brown it all over. Turn it carefully, with two spoons, so it won't fall apart. Pour in about 125ml stock. Cover with a lid, reduce the heat, and cook over a low heat for 40 minutes. Turn the loaf a couple of times.

let's make...
SAUSAGES &
SAUERKRAUT

Sausages are a typical midweek supper dish, but they are also everyone's favourite at a Sunday barbecue. You can find them on stands at Christmas markets or at funfairs too.

WHAT YOU NEED:

SERVES 4-6 PEOPLE:

1 onion
1 tablespoon lard or
    cooking oil (plus
    more oil for frying)
675g sauerkraut
125ml apple juice
3 juniper berries
salt, black pepper
24 cocktail sausages (approx
    25g each; or 4–6 large
    sausages)

◁ There are about
1,500 different types of
    sausages in Germany!
I love the ones from
Nuremberg best.

WHAT'S THIS: _sauerkraut?_

This is a sliced and fermented or soured cabbage. It is popular in Germany and Poland.

MY TIP

Sausages are great with ketchup or mustard. In Berlin, people eat them with a curry sauce – that's ketchup with curry powder stirred in. Delicious!

1 Peel and chop the onion *(see page 5)*. In a saucepan heat the lard or oil. Add the onion and fry for 5 minutes over a medium heat, until the onion is transparent (see-through).

2 Add the sauerkraut and fork through with two forks to loosen it. Then pour in the apple juice and stir in the juniper berries. Season with salt and pepper, and cook uncovered over a low heat for about 30 minutes.

3 While the sauerkraut is cooking, heat a little oil in a frying pan (or light a barbecue). Add the sausages and cook over a medium heat for about 10 minutes. Turn them a few times to ensure they are browned evenly all over.

4 Serve the sauerkraut with the sausages and some mashed potatoes or potato salad.

let's make...
RED GROATS

Everyone just loves this fruit dessert. You can find it in the simplest homes and in the most expensive restaurants. Originally, it comes from northern Germany.

WHAT YOU NEED:

MAKES 8 PORTIONS:

500g redcurrants
100g cherries
100g raspberries
225g trawberries
2–4 tablespoons sugar

300g redcurrant jelly
or cherry jam
1 cinnamon stick
2 tablespoons cornflour

FOR THE SAUCE:

2 vanilla pods
800ml milk
2 tablespoons sugar
1½ tablespoons
cornflour
2 egg yolks
½ cup whipping
or double cream

◁ Originally, this recipe was always made using only red fruits, but I've made a green version with gooseberries and kiwis, and my brother made a yellow one with peaches and pineapple.

WHAT'S THIS: groats?

Rote grütze, or red groats, was originally made with crushed grains called groats and fruit juice. This version is still cooked in eastern Europe. But today, a much lighter version is made with cornflour and fresh fruit, and this is popular everywhere.

1 Wash the redcurrants and pull them off their stalks with a fork. Wash the cherries; remove the stalks and pits. Don't wash the raspberries but pick over and throw away any that are mouldy. Wash the strawberries, pull off the green stems, and cut the fruits in halves or quarters, if they are large.

2 In a large saucepan, combine 2 tablespoons sugar, the fruit jelly or jam and the cinnamon, then bring to the boil. Add the redcurrants and cherries, and cook for about 2–3 minutes. **!**

3 In a bowl, stir the cornflour into a little cold water. Stir this into the saucepan. Cook and stir until the mixture begins to thicken. **!**

4 Now add in the raspberries and strawberries. Add sugar to taste, stir, then let the mixture cool. **!**

6 Take the saucepan off the heat. In a bowl, whisk together the egg yolks and the cream. Pour this mixture into the vanilla milk. Don't boil it again. Allow to cool. **!**

5 Meanwhile slit open the vanilla pods and scrape out the seeds. In a saucepan, bring the seeds, pods, milk and sugar to a boil. In a bowl, stir the cornflour into a little water until smooth. Add this to the milk and cook briefly until it thickens.

Look it up
GERMANY

advent the four weeks before Christmas; German children have countdown advent calendars and families lights candles on their advent wreaths

carnival the time before Lent; marked by wearing costumes and masks, joining processions and many celebrations

dirndl traditional folk clothes of a woman in Bavaria; a skirt, blouse and apron

groats a hulled and crushed cereal

kaffee und kuchen coffee and cake; a favourite German afternoon meal

lederhosen traditional folk clothes for a man in Bavaria; three-quarter-length trousers or shorts, made from leather

Lent the period of fasting before Easter for devout Christians

mutzenmandeln a favourite biscuit baked and eaten during carnival

Oktoberfest a beer festival in Munich; the largest festival in the world

polterabend the eve of a wedding in Germany; friends smash their old china on the couple's doorstep, and the couple has to sweep up the shards

sauerbraten a pickled pot roast of beef; the meat is marinated in a vinegar sauce for several days; originally sauerbraten was made with horse meat

sauerkraut a pickled cabbage; can be eaten hot or cold

St Martin (316–397 CE) a Roman soldier and later the Bishop of Tours in France; known as the patron saint of France; his acts of kindness are celebrated by lantern processions on 11 November in Germany

stollen a German Christmas cake; it is shaped with a dent down its length, to resemble the swaddling clothes of the baby Jesus

Find out more
GERMANY

Books to read

Amos, Janine
Germany and German (Countrywise)
Chrysalis Children's Books: 2003

Lord, Richard and McKay, Susan
Germany: Festivals of the World
Heinemann Library, 1996

Sheen, Barbara
Foods of Germany
KidHaven Press, 2006

Spengler, Kremena
Germany: A Question and Answer Book
Fact Finders, 2004

Web sites to check out

www.germany.info/relaunch/culture/life/ G_Kids/index.htm
The kids' pages of the Web site of the German Embassy in Washington, D.C.

www.cia.gov/library/publications/the- world-factbook/geos/gm.html
The CIA's site with information, facts and figures about Germany

www.germanculture.com.ua
A site all about German culture, history, sports and daily life, with lots of information on food and festivals

www.globalgourmet.com/destinations/ germany
All about food in northern, central and southern Germany, festivals and feasts

www.travelsthroughgermany.com/ website2/germanfood.htm
Recipes and feature articles on German food and culture

Index

GERMANY